From InDesign CS 5.5 to EPUB and Kindle
A Straight to the Point Miniguide

Written and illustrated by Elizabeth Castro
http://www.elizabethcastro.com/epub
Copyright © 2012 by Elizabeth Castro. All rights reserved.

Cover image modeled in Cheetah3D, Blender, and Photoshop by Andreu Cabré
http://andreucabre.blogspot.com

Published by Cookwood Press
http://www.cookwood.com

Many thanks to *Cari Jansen* and *Anne-Marie Concepción* who read through this book and offered helpful suggestions and corrections.

ISBN:

Print: 978-1-61150-020-2

EPUB: 978-1-61150-018-9

Kindle: 978-1-61150-019-6

From InDesign CS 5.5 to EPUB and Kindle

Right now there are a lot of tools on the market for creating ebooks. There is only one, however, that is useful for creating both professional-quality print books *and* ebooks. That program, of course, is Adobe InDesign. If you have a lot of existing files in InDesign or you're planning on selling both print and digital versions of your books, having a single workflow for a large part of the process can save a lot of time.

The latest version of the InDesign software, CS 5.5, has a number of improvements over earlier versions though it still has some room to grow. I'll show you how to prepare your documents for the most effective conversion to the two major ebook formats—first to EPUB for the great majority of ereaders, including iPad, iPhone, and iPod touch, and then from EPUB to Kindle/mobi for Amazon Kindle.

This is not a beginner's guide to InDesign or ebook creation. Instead, I'll be explaining how to get the most out of the new features that have been recently added to CS 5.5 that have to do with creating EPUB format ebooks, and what you need to do to convert those EPUBs into valid Kindle/mobi format books for Amazon Kindle. I will assume you have some basic knowledge of both InDesign and EPUB.

If you want more background on EPUB, I recommend my companion guide, *EPUB Straight to the Point: Creating ebooks for the Apple iPad and other ereaders*, which thoroughly covers the EPUB format itself.

Also note that there is a very important EPUB-related update to InDesign CS 5.5. To install, choose Help > Updates and follow the instructions you'll find there.

Table of Contents

InDesign to ebook in 10 steps

Going from InDesign to EPUB is a straightforward process. I'll list the steps here and then go into them in more detail in the sections that follow.

1 Learn what InDesign can and cannot do. (See "Envisioning your book" on page 7.)

2 Design your book and create a template or sample chapter with all of the styles you'll need. (See "Creating your book in InDesign" on page 17.)

3 Create your book—in one or more documents—and apply styles to format the book's contents. (See "Creating your book in InDesign" on page 17.)

4 Add any special features desired, including images, audio and video, and links, cross references and footnotes.

5 Create a table of contents style.

6 Deciding how InDesign should convert its paragraph and character styles into HTML and CSS.

7 Add pertinent metadata so that your book can be found by readers and booksellers.

8 Export the file to EPUB, taking care to choose the appropriate settings, in order to add additional metadata, create a cover, choose the desired export order, maintain image formatting, generate the CSS properly, and much more.

9 If you're not satisfied with InDesign's result, crack open the EPUB and modify the HTML and CSS by hand, for example, to prepare for conversion to Kindle/mobi or to ensure that embedded fonts are properly displayed.

10 Convert to Kindle/mobi format, if desired.

Envisioning your book

Before you begin, you should understand how print books and ebooks differ as well as InDesign's strengths and weaknesses in creating each format. In this section, I'll go over what is possible in EPUB and Kindle/mobi formats, and how much of that InDesign can do on its own.

You're probably already familiar with print books and how InDesign creates them. You create a master page with elements that should appear on each page. You then create individual pages and control the position of the text and graphics on each page. You create paragraph and character styles to control the font, size, margins, and other characteristics of the text. And when you finish, you print out pages that look precisely like what you see on screen.

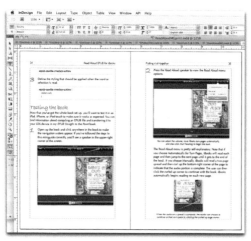

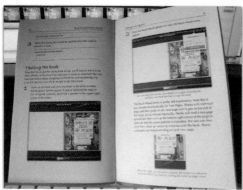

The InDesign document is identical to the printed edition.

As you probably already know, an ebook is a different kind of fish altogether. Instead of being contained in a physical page, an ebook is an amorphous stream of content that can fit into different size recipients (from iPad to Kindle Fire to iPhone) and even change sizes itself.

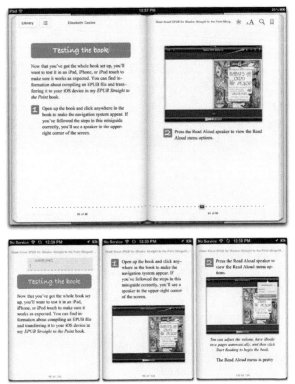

The corresponding EPUB file looks different in different ereaders, as it is reflowed, and the font-size is changed (iPad top, iPhone bottom).

This makes ebooks extremely flexible. Indeed, ebook formats are modeled after the same language—HTML—in which web pages are written and which was designed to be universally compatible with any browser on any operating system.

But that same flexibility requires the designer to give up a lot of control, particularly over positioning. No longer can you insist that a particular bit of content appear below an image (as with a caption), on page 3, or on a left hand page, or even in many cases at the top of the page. Instead, you have to be satisfied with relative control: the biggest headers should be three times as big as the body text, the image should be as wide as the page, and so on.

On the other hand, ebooks can do some things print books just cannot: contain links, audio and video, and even interactive elements.

If you want your print book and ebooks to resemble each other, you may want to study what is possible in an ebook (a moving target, but not impossible) and tailor your print book to use these characteristics, and also avoid effects that you can only achieve in print. (Of course, you may also decide to embrace the benefits of each format and allow them to diverge.)

What can you do in an ebook?

And can InDesign do it for you? Even though this section of the book couldn't possibly be current by the time you read it, most of it will be. Cutting-edge features are few. This section will give you a feel for what is generally possible in an ebook, and whether InDesign is capable of creating those effects. Also see "Converting to Kindle/mobi".

Running headers/footers

These are the lines of text that appear at the top or bottom of every page in a print book. Sometimes they change from chapter to chapter or section to section, sometimes they stay the same throughout a book. In most ereaders, the only running header or footer comes from the title of the book and is generated automatically, displayed as part of the navigational tools, and can be hidden from sight. The ebook designer cannot change the running header or footer from chapter to chapter, nor change its position or style. InDesign does not export running headers or footers, nor anything else from the Master Pages.

Page numbers

In a print book, where the number of pages is always the same, page numbers are permanently marked on each page. In an ebook whose text may be magnified or reduced in size, page numbers are variable. Some ereaders show different page numbers depending on the current size of the text and pagination of the book, some link page numbers to the page numbers in the original print book, and some offer percentages or word counts.

InDesign does not export page numbers, nor does it mark the boundaries of the print page for reference in the ebook.

Fonts

In a print book, the designer chooses one or more fonts for the text and these cannot be altered by the reader. In addition, the designer buys the font once from the font foundry and is not charged additional fees for using it in any number of copies of any number of books.

Most ereaders have a limited set of built-in fonts in which a book can be displayed. Some ereaders allow font embedding but careful attention must be paid to each font's licensing to ensure that embedding is allowed and that additional fees are not incurred. Generally, even the ereaders that allow font embedding will allow the user to override the designers' choices and revert to default fonts.

InDesign lets you choose any font that you want for both print and ebooks. Unfortunately, it doesn't embed fonts in a way that iBooks supports. I explain how to adjust the code so that iBooks can display the fonts in "Using embedded fonts in iBooks" on page 73. Kindle does not currently support font embedding at all.

Text size

In a print book, the designer chooses the size of the headers, body text, captions, and any other text in the book. These cannot be changed by the reader.

In an ebook, the designer chooses the initial size of the text, but generally the user can increase or decrease the text size. All the text is altered simultaneously so that the relative sizes stay the same. That is, if the header starts 3 times bigger than the body text, it will still be 3 times bigger than the body text even if both are reduced 25%.

InDesign exports text sizes using the font-size property. It takes the point size specified in InDesign and converts them to ems at a rate of 12 points per em. So, for 12 pt text, the CSS would be font-size: 1em. Note that Kindle discourages setting the font size for the body text.

Other text formatting

The designer can add all sorts of formatting to the text, including italics, bold, underlining, color, shadows, kerning, and more. Most of this formatting is maintained in ebooks as well and cannot be changed by the user. Some ereaders are limited with respect to how much formatting they can show. For example, black and white ereaders obviously cannot show color, but many are also unable to show kerning, shadows, or other advanced text formatting.

InDesign exports bold, italic, and bold italic styles as expected, with the font-weight and font-style properties, respectively. In CS 5.5, if desired, you can map character styles to the em or strong tags. InDesign exports underlining (specified with the underline property in the Character dialog box) using the text-decoration: underline property value pair. It exports strikethrough with text-decoration : line-through. InDesign completely ignores the options for Rule Above and Rule Below.

InDesign does export information about the color of characters, with the expected color property and a hex value for the color. It does not export information for the outline color of text.

The small caps, all caps, subscript and superscript are all properly exported: with font-variant: small-caps, text-transform: uppercase, vertical-align: super, and vertical-align: sub (and not <sup> or <sub>), respectively.

Spacing, page breaks, and orphans

In a print book, the designer chooses the amount of space between lines and paragraphs, the size of the margins, how much space should come after headers, where page breaks should or should not occur, and whether or not widows and orphans should be allowed, and to what degree.

In an ebook, some but not all of that spacing can be controlled. Line-height is always a relative value and waxes and wanes with the size of the text. InDesign calculates the ratio of the specified leading with respect to the specified font-size and uses the result as the value for line-height. For example, the CSS for 12pt text with 16pt leading would be line-height: 1.33 (16/12).

InDesign exports the values specified for Space Before, Right Indent, Space After, and Left Indent, in that order and converted to pixels, with the margin property. 1 pixel is equivalent to 1/72 of an inch, 0.35mm, 1 point, and 1/12 of a pica. So if Space Before was 6mm, Right Indent was .5in, Space After was 6pt, and Left Indent was 6px, InDesign's CSS would look like: margin: 17px 36px 6px 6px;. InDesign does not apply padding.

You can use InDesign's First Line Indent to start the first line of a paragraph either within or outside the rest of the paragraph. Negative values are allowed. InDesign converts all units to pixels (see previous paragraph) and uses the result for the value of text-indent.

InDesign has powerful settings in its Keep Options dialog box which it unfortunately does not export to EPUB. These options control page breaks, keep certain paragraphs together, and control how many lines of a paragraph can sit alone at the top or bottom of a page by themselves. Most of these features can be recreated with the CSS properties page-break-before, page-break-after, and page-break-inside, but InDesign does not yet do so. You can crack open the EPUB yourself to add them. (See "How do you crack open an EPUB?" on page 65.)

Alignment

Most professionally typeset books have justified text. It looks good thanks to the extensive kerning and tracking options, and language-specific hyphenations options offered by programs such as InDesign.

Ebooks are not so lucky. Many ereaders have rudimentary hyphenation systems, often just for the System language, and impose ereader-wide justification settings regardless of what the designer selected.

Enter InDesign. For print it offers a variety of features for controlling text alignment, from left, right, center, and justify, to justify left, justify right, justify center and full justify. Only the first four are exported to EPUB, and unfortunately, even these four are not always observed by ereaders. iBooks in particular insists on full justification by default, and hides the setting in the General Settings outside iBooks. This full justification overrides any designer-selected rules, unless you use hack the code as described in "Controlling Text Alignment" in *EPUB Straight to the Point*.

Columns

Columns make perfect sense if you have enough room for them on the printed page. With a flexible layout and the potential for a screen that's two inches wide, they can be a disaster. InDesign does not export columns.

Drop caps and all caps

A print designer often chooses to display the first letter of a chapter with a drop cap and the entire line that follows in all caps. This is also possible in ebooks.

InDesign has a nice drop cap feature that exports to EPUB by isolating the letter(s) that should be enlarged and then applies floats and margin adjustments to make them fit into the surrounding text. Unfortunately, it doesn't apply this formatting to the Drop cap style, if you've created one, but rather to a generic selector created on the fly.

Although InDesign has nested line styles that can format the first line in all caps (for example), this information is not exported to EPUB. You can adjust that by hand by cracking open the EPUB and editing the CSS.

Non-Latin characters and other symbols

A print book can contain characters from any language, in any direction, and any symbol that is required. In contrast, some ereaders are limited to only the Latin character set, and can only be set left-to-right. Others, and certainly most in the future, will be able to have text go right-to-left and vertically.

Currently InDesign exports EPUB in UTF-8 format, which means that foreign alphabets and characters are exported correctly. The only symbols that need special care are any that you've set with Zapf Dingbats.

Images

Both print books and ebooks can have images, but there is much more control over the placement of images in print books. In a print book, the designer specifies the exact location on a particular page where the image should go. In an ebook, the designer chooses the text before or after which the image should appear, but depending on the size of the text, it might be in any part of any page.

Text can wrap around images in both print and ebooks, but because some ereaders are so narrow, it is not always a feasible choice for the latter.

Finally, color images can make a print book much more expensive while they have little effect on the cost of an ebook. On the other hand, some ereaders are not capable of showing images in color.

InDesign CS5.5 offers extensive control over how you export images to EPUB. You can choose the format, size, and resolution of your images and InDesign now automatically formats wrapped text around images correctly. I'll explain the details in "Options when exporting images".

Borders and background colors

In print books, any combination of borders and background colors is possible, though the use of color can make a print book considerably more expensive to produce. In an ebook, some ereaders allow borders around text or images and background colors for pages or objects like sidebars, but support varies widely from one ereader to the next.

InDesign doesn't export any borders or background colors. If you want to use them, you have to add them manually by cracking open the EPUB and adjusting the CSS.

Table of contents and index

A print book generally has a table of contents at the beginning and an index at the end, with page number references in each. Ebooks have two kinds of tables of contents: a (required) *navigational* table of contents that appears in the menus of the ereader, and an optional, more conventional *inline* table of contents in the body of the ebook.

Ebooks can also have indexes, but instead of referring a reader to a particular page, since none exist, the index will simply link directly to the given destination. Ereaders also let readers search any phrase, whether or not it's part of an organized index.

InDesign has powerful table of contents and indexing tools for print books, but only some of that power is available for ebooks. When you export from InDesign, it will export any tables of contents that you have created, but only the first one will contain linked references. As for the index, it simply skips it altogether. I have a blog post on *Pigs, Gourds, and Wikis* that explains how to create a linked index.

Hyphenation

Print affords the designer complete control over hyphenation. Designers often adjust the spacing of lines of text or individual words to ensure that enough but not too much hyphenation is used and that the words in the rest of the paragraph have the proper spacing. There are very distinct rules of hyphenation for different languages.

For some unknown reason, ereaders don't yet allow the same level of control over hyphenation. First, I have yet to see an ereader that can distinguish between two different languages in a single ebook, or even one that pays attention to settings in the EPUB when using more than one language. iBooks even gets hyphenation wrong in English on an English system (though it mostly gets it right). But there's no guarantee for multilingual documents. Kindle has no hyphenation at all.

A designer can choose to disallow hyphenation completely (for example, in a header) or to depend on the vagaries of each ereader in which the ebook is displayed.

InDesign supports hyphenation to the nth degree, but unfortunately does not export that information to EPUB. You can, however, edit the EPUB files to exert some control over hyphenation yourself, for those ereaders that support it.

Links

In a print book, it's common to refer a reader to another page with "see page 245" or "consult Chapter 3, *Working with images*", or even "check her website: http://www.elizabethcastro.com". In an ebook, since page numbers don't exist, it makes more sense to create hyperlinks to specific sections of a book.

InDesign helps you create *hyperlinks*, in which you have to designate both the text for the link as well as its destination—which might be inside the book or outside on a website—*cross references*, in which the text for the link comes directly from the text in the destination, and *footnotes*, that link to a source or other information about the text.

InDesign exports links to EPUB (and thus to Kindle/mobi), as expected. A bug in InDesign CS 5 in which some links were broken has thankfully been fixed in InDesign CS 5.5.

Tables

Tables are a key ingredient to many print books but in ebooks they suffer from the same issue as columns and text wrap: there is often simply not enough room for them on the screen. A table's rigidity is its downfall since it can't adapt to smaller areas or smaller screens. Some ereaders let you display tables full screen but others break them up or squash them into the screen. InDesign creates tables very well, and exports them with standard HTML code, but doesn't do anything special to help adapt them to smaller screens.

Audio and video

There are some print books with audio and video add-ons—a book with bird calls comes to mind—but they require an additional device to make them work. Ebooks can have audio and video incorporated into the page, but not all ereaders can handle them. It's a good idea to have fallback solutions in those ebooks in which audio and video fail. You can now export audio and video from InDesign to EPUB. See "Placing and exporting audio and video" on page 35 for details and caveats.

Currently, only Apple allows independent publishers to add audio and video to their ebooks. For awhile it looked like Amazon supported embedded audio and video as well, though only in Kindle apps on iOS (!), but now they don't even allow that. Barnes & Noble's NOOK Color supports audio and video but won't accept such files submitted by independent publishers.

Creating your book in InDesign

Once you know what you can do with InDesign, you can prepare the design of your book. I generally do this step by placing a sample chapter in an InDesign document of the proper size for the print edition, and then by defining paragraph, character, and object styles.

It's fine to include features that only work in print or only work in digital, as long as you're aware that they'll only work in one or the other formats. For example, it's perfectly reasonable to create master pages and master page items, say for running heads or page numbers for the print edition, just as long as you keep in mind that they will not appear in the EPUB or Kindle/mobi editions of your book.

Apart from the actual appearance of your book—which will be defined by the styles that you create—you should also decide whether to create a single document for your entire book or to divide your book into multiple documents, perhaps for individual chapters. Either way is fine. While earlier versions of InDesign favored one system or another, I think it's safe to say that you can now choose the system that is most comfortable for you, and it won't greatly affect the ebook versions of your work. That said, unless your book is extremely small, I recommend creating an InDesign book to organize the contents into multiple documents. InDesign books are handy when working with very large books as they let you work with smaller, more agile chapters. It's also true that some numbering and section options are only available when you have separate documents. Finally separate InDesign documents always start on a new page in an ebook. This is still the only foolproof method for creating a page break.

To create a book, choose File > New > Book, give the book a file name and then click the plus sign in the new Book panel to add chapters to your book.

It's important to designate a Style Source for your book by clicking to the left of the ID icon and chapter name in the Book panel. The Style Source is the chapter that is used to generate the table of contents, and its styles are the ones copied to the rest of your book when you choose Synchronize Book in the Book panel menu.

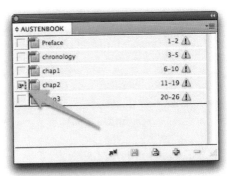

The document with the little icon filled in to the left indicates which file is the Style Source for your book.

Creating a template

A template is nothing more than a sample chapter that includes all of the styles that you will need throughout your book. If you created a sample chapter while designing your book, that file may work fine as a template. You can always add to a template as you progress through the book, since sometimes it's not until later that you realize you need a new style for a particular situation.

Saving a template

You can save a template in a special format to keep from making changes to it inadvertently by going to File > Save As and choosing InDesign Template in the Format menu. That said, if, like me, you find you're constantly updating your template, it can be easier to treat one of the live chapters of your book as the template. Then you can add styles to the chapter, and simply re-import the styles to the rest of your book's chapters.

To import styles from one document to another, choose Load Paragraph Styles from the Paragraph Styles panel menu and then choose the template chapter that contains the desired styles.

To import styles from a template chapter into *all* of the other chapters of the book, open the Book panel, and make sure the template chapter is specified as the Style Source for your book.

Then choose Synchronize Book from the Books panel menu. As long as the appropriate options are chosen in the Synchronize Options dialog box, the styles from the Style Source document will be copied to all of the other documents in your book.

The importance of styles

Styles are the key to formatting both print and ebooks in InDesign. Styles let you tag an entire collection of content and format it in one fell swoop. In addition, styles in InDesign are almost analogous with styles in EPUB, so by applying styles in InDesign you make it easier to control and format your ebooks as well.

All major ebook formats are based on HTML, the same language that web pages are written in. HTML is an ingenious system of *marking* (that's the *M* in HTML) different parts of your content to identify what each one is. So a <p> tag might identify a paragraph and an <h1> tag might identify a top level heading. If you're used to working with InDesign, you may think this looks very familiar to styles, and you'd be right.

There are some slight differences. In InDesign you define styles for paragraphs, characters, and even objects, by specifying the formatting that should be applied to each one. In HTML, you first specify what kind of content something is (a paragraph, a division, an image, etc.), then you identify particular instances of those elements (say, all of the "bodytext" paragraphs, or perhaps all of the "photo" images), and finally, in an accompanying style sheet, you define the formatting that should be applied to those elements.

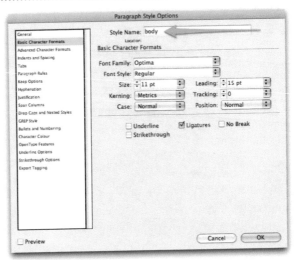

Here's some of the definition of the body *style in InDesign.*

When InDesign exports a file to EPUB, it creates p elements with the name of the style of each paragraph as a class, by default. In CS 5.5, you can customize how paragraph and character styles are converted to HTML and CSS. I'll show you how in "Mapping tags to export" on page 44.

```
121 ▼  p.body {
122         font-family : Optima, sans-serif;
123         font-weight : normal;
124         font-style : normal;
125         font-size : 0.92em;
126         text-decoration : none;
127         font-variant : normal;
128         line-height : 1.36;
129         text-align : left;
130         color : #000000;
131         text-indent : 0px;
132         margin : 0px 0px 6px 0px;
133     }
```

InDesign converts the style definition of the body *style into a CSS selector applied to* p *elements with class* body.

The way in which you apply styles depends a bit on where the content comes from originally. If you're importing documents that already contain formatting, you'll want to maintain as much of that as is useful. If you import plain text documents, I recommend applying a body style to the entire document at once, and then applying styles to the headers, captions, images, and other special elements individually.

Creating a cover

One of InDesign CS 5.5's most notable improvements is that you can now associate a cover with the exported EPUB. And although you generate the file during the actual export process, it's a good idea to prepare the content of your cover ahead of time.

InDesign can either generate a cover image from the contents of the first page of your book or document, or you can link to an external image that you've prepared elsewhere, perhaps in Photoshop. Let's look at the first system.

Generating a cover from the first page

One of the advantages of creating a cover right in your InDesign document is that it will automatically have the same proportions as your ebook. This is not required, but it probably makes sense. Note that cover images do not all have to be a standard size. On iBooks, they must be at least 600 pixels wide along the larger axis. On a Nook, I recommend 600 x 800px. Kindle requires that the dimensions be at least 500 x 800 pixels and recommends a height/width ratio of 1.6.

1   Place the images and text that should be included in your cover on the first page of your first InDesign document.

Remember that the cover of an ebook is rarely displayed full size. More often, only a tiny representation of it is shown, either on an ebook commerce site like Amazon or Apple's iBookstore or in the bookshelf on an ereader. So, it's important to make sure that your cover works at a small size. To that end, you can adjust the cover so that extraneous text and images are removed and that the title and author are a bit bigger than might be warranted in print.

This cover is made up of a background image and two text frames.

You could stop here and just use the Export options that I'll explain later to generate your cover. The problem is that while InDesign will create a *cover image* for you from the first page of your book, it will only use that image in iBooks opposite the table of contents and as an icon in the iBookstore. However it won't use it as the first page of your book. Instead, it will output the contents of the page individually: first the two text frames, then the image. The special font that I've used here will either require special treatment, or be ignored altogether.

The first page of your book does not look like the original cover.

The solution is to group the individual pieces of your book and then have InDesign rasterize them (convert them to a single image) both for the cover and for the first page.

2 Select all the parts of the cover and choose Object > Group. You will see a dotted line around the image and the text frames.

3 Next, choose Object > Object Export Options. In the dialog box that appears, choose the EPUB and HTML tab. Then check Custom Rasterization, Custom Image Alignment and Spacing, and Insert Page Break (After Image). (For help choosing a Size and Resolution, see "Options when exporting images" on page 54.)

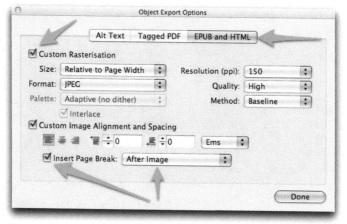

These options will make InDesign create a single image file out of your image and text. Normally, Apple won't permit you to include text in an image, but it's OK and even expected for a cover. When you check the Insert Page Break (After Image) option, you ensure that the cover image will be placed on its own page. Don't create a page break before the image, as that would generate a blank page at the beginning of your book.

4 Finally, click Done.

Now your first page will work as both the cover image and the first page of your book once you are ready to Export to EPUB (and later to Kindle/mobi) as described in "Exporting to EPUB".

Note: I have noticed that InDesign sometimes adds extra white space around images that have been cropped or large text blocks. You may need to adjust accordingly.

Placing images and controlling export order

InDesign CS 5.5 gives you three choices about how to control the order of the elements on the printed page when converted into an ebook. I'm only going to talk about the first and last, Based on Page Layout and Based on Articles Panel. For more info on using XML with InDesign, I recommend reading Cari Jansen's blog post: http://carijansen.com/2010/09/18/moving-print-publications-to-epub/

InDesign's default method of exporting content is to begin at the left-most, topmost frame on the first page, export its *entire* contents—regardless of how many frames or pages it appears on—and then continue on with the next item down until it reaches the bottom of the page. It then continues with the next left most object. For very simple layouts, like novels, this may work just fine. For more complicated layouts, you may be surprised at how the exported EPUB is ordered. For long passages of text with intermittent graphic elements, your best option for controlling the order of the contents in an ebook is with anchored objects—either inline or custom positioned.

The new system of Articles InDesign CS 5.5 offers an additional alternative for controlling export order. You can assign text frames and images to an article and then reorder the elements within an article, as well as rearrange the articles themselves, until you're satisfied with the export order. This can be very useful when you have short text frames, but it doesn't help with placing images in specific locations in a long block of text.

Using inline objects to control export order

If your layout is relatively simple, but with long bits of text, the best way to control the order in which images or other elements appear in your exported ebook is by placing them right into the flow of the text in your InDesign document. If you place them after a given paragraph in your print book, that's where they'll appear in the ebook as well.

(Note that I will be talking about images in this section, but you can use most of these techniques for independent text frames—like pull quotes—as well.)

Let's look at a quick example. Here is a very simply laid out book. The image is placed in an independent graphic frame.

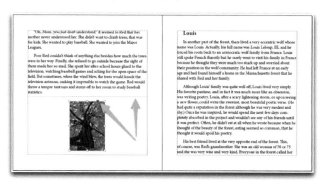

The solid blue box at the right end of the top edge indicates that the image is in an independent graphic frame. Notice how the text frame does not contain the graphic.

When we export this book with the "Based on Page Layout" option, InDesign exports all the text in the entire story, and then places the image at the end. That's not what we want. What we want is for that tree image to always appear just after the paragraph in the story about the trees. The solution is to create an inline image—the simplest kind of anchored object—that flows with the text and whose content is exported together with the text.

I like to create a special format for the paragraph that will contain the inline image, both so I can adjust the leading in my print book as well as adjust the formatting in the resulting ebook.

1. Create a style for inline elements. I call mine "illustration". Be sure that the illustration's style's leading is set to Auto so that the paragraph expands with the height of the illustration. You can also adjust the Space Before and Space After fields as desired.

2. Place the cursor where you want to insert your image. Press Return, then use the up arrow to return to your new paragraph and style it with your illustration style.

3. Choose File > Place and select the image that you wish to place in your book.

You can resize, crop, rotate, add space around, or otherwise modify the image as desired. Upon export, you can tell InDesign to maintain these changes for the EPUB document, or to ignore them. (See "Options when exporting images" on page 54 for details.)

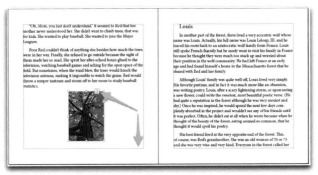

An inline graphic displays an anchor symbol when you select it.
Note also that the text frame encloses the inline graphic.

This time, when you export this document to EPUB, the image will appear after the same paragraph that it followed in your InDesign document.

Tip

If you're converting a print book into ebook format and already have all of the images placed, you can quickly slide an image inline by selecting it, holding down the Shift key, and dragging the blue square in the upper right corner to the desired location in the text.

Custom positioned anchored objects

Inline anchored objects don't give you much control over their placement in the print edition of your book. They flow along as if they were just one more paragraph of text. If you're interested in wrapping text around objects, or if the objects are already placed and you simply want to control where they appear in your exported text, I recommend using what InDesign calls *custom positioned anchored objects*. InDesign CS 5.5 makes it really easy to create a custom positioned anchored object from an existing object—placed practically anywhere on the page—and to link it to the bit of text that it should appear next to upon export.

For this example, imagine that we start with a text frame that has an independent image sitting on top of it with text wrap applied.

1   Click the image to select it and view the anchor box on the top right corner.

The solid blue box at the right end of the top edge indicates that the image is not anchored.

2   Drag the blue anchor box to the spot in the text where you wish it to appear when exported to EPUB. We'll drag it right before the first word in the paragraph.

Drag the solid blue box to the beginning of the paragraph that should flow around it.

The image's position on the page does not change, but now the blue box turns into a blue anchor to show that the image is anchored in the text and will be exported at the point in the text where it is anchored. If it has text wrap applied as in this example, the text wrap will also be maintained in the EPUB file.

The solid blue box at the right end of the top edge indicates that the image is not anchored.

⋙ Tips ⋘

Note that you can't anchor an image with text wrapped around it to a spot that's *after* the location of the image itself. If you do, the text wrap is eliminated.

If you hold down the Shift key while you drag the blue box, the image is automatically converted to an inline object and placed at the insertion point.

When we export to EPUB, the image is where we want it—embedded in the text.

An anchored image around which text is flowed will be exported as a floating image in the EPUB file. Unfortunately, the space around it is not maintained.

If you want to add a little space around the image, you can go into the EPUB file and adjust the CSS, or as long as you choose Preserve Appearance from Layout when you export to EPUB, you can adjust the spacing in InDesign, and the space will be preserved.

Using articles to control export order

With InDesign CS 5.5, you have an added tool in your toolbox for controlling the order of exported items, the Articles panel. An article is a named collection of one or more text frames, images, or other objects. Your document can have multiple articles. Once you've defined your articles, you can set the export order of the contents of an ebook by rearranging the elements in an article or by rearranging the articles themselves. It can be very helpful.

Note, however, that articles can only control the order of *entire* text threads, images, or other objects. You can't specify that a given image be exported after a particular position in an accompanying story. It must either go before the whole story or after the whole story. In addition, if you have inline images or sidebars—anchored within a story, as described in the previous sections—you won't be able to change the order of those objects in the Articles panel. They will always be exported with the text in which they appear. For more granular control, see the previous sections on "Using inline objects to control export order" and "Custom positioned anchored objects" .

Here is a book of articles about crazy weather. Notice how there are six frames on the page, two photos and four text articles.

If you export this document to InDesign with the default "Based on Page Layout" option, you may be surprised and probably disappointed at how things are ordered in the resulting EPUB.

First we see the body of the text, since it is the left most item in the layout in InDesign:

The body of the text is exported first since it was the left-most item.

Next, we see the rest of the stories output in left to right order:

This is not how we want the content ordered in the ebook.

For this example, let's say that we want the larger right hand image to come first, followed by the headline, the body of the article, and then the author byline. We want to eliminate "New England News" from the export entirely. And we really want the smaller image to be embedded in the text itself.

1   The first step is to open the Articles panel by choosing Window > Articles.

The Articles panel starts out empty. You have to add articles to it manually either by dragging frames to it or by clicking the plus sign.

You can either drag individual frames, stories, or images to the Articles panel or Command-click (Control-click on PC) to add all of the elements on the current page to the Articles panel.

Note that an article is not equivalent to a text frame or an image, but is more like a folder that can contain a series of text threads or images.

2   Command-click the plus sign in the Articles panel to add all of the elements on the page to a single article in the Articles panel, or Shift-click each article individually before clicking the plus sign to add them in the order they were selected. (Thanks @carijansen!).

3   In the Article Options box that appears, give the article a name and check the Include When Exporting box.

The name that you choose for the article is used as the class name for the div in the exported EPUB file.

The stories are added to a single article in the Articles panel. Notice that when you select an element, for example, the image in the upper right of the screen, a blue square appears next to that image in the Articles panel.

Each one of the elements on the page is listed in the Snowtober article in the Articles panel.

4   Now that the elements are listed, we can order them as we wish, simply by dragging. We want the larger image first, followed by the title and the author's byline, followed by the body text.

You can reorder the elements in the Articles panel without affecting how they are displayed on the page.

Eliminate items from the article that you don't want to include in the EPUB file by selecting them and clicking the trash can. We'll eliminate the New England News header.

Eliminate individual stories from the export by selecting them and clicking the garbage can. You can keep an entire article from being included by unchecking its name.

 Export the document to EPUB being careful to choose Same as Articles panel under Ordering in the General tab of the EPUB Export Options dialog box.

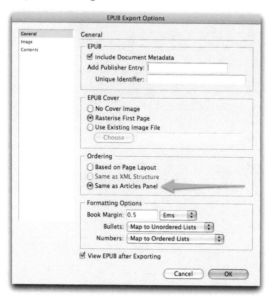

Don't forget to choose Same as Articles panel in the EPUB Export Options dialog box.

Now when you export this document to EPUB, the order is much closer to what we want. (I'll go over Export options in more detail in "Exporting to EPUB" on page 49.)

Now the stories in the InDesign document are exported the way we want, and the header is not included.

⇒ Tips ⇐

It's important to note that once you anchor an image to a specific location in a body of text, you can't change its export order in the Articles panel—indeed it won't even appear in the Articles panel. It becomes a part of the text item and is exported together with that text.

Or, put another way, you can only reorder independent text items and images.

Placing and exporting audio and video

With version 5.5 of InDesign comes the ability to export any placed audio or video files into an EPUB document.

You can place an audio or video file in the usual way (File > Place) or by opening the Media panel and clicking the little filmstrip in the bottom right corner. InDesign currently supports .mp3 and .mp4 media files only. Once the media file is placed (and still selected), you can set options for it in that same Media panel.

Click the film at the bottom-right to place a video or audio file.

Check the Play on Page Load box to have the media file play automatically when the reader gets to the page that contains it. Earlier versions of iBooks did not allow audio or video to play automatically, but from at least version 1.3.2 on, it does. Note however, that iBooks is not very consistent about when it plays an audio file. Sometimes it plays automatically when you open the book, sometimes when you get to the page that contains the audio. Whether you choose Stop on Page Turn or not, iBooks does not currently stop the audio unless you press the pause button.

Check the Loop box to have the media file repeat from the beginning
each time it reaches the end.

*For video, don't forget to choose (any!) option for Controller so that
InDesign includes the controls and your readers can turn your video
on and off.*

If you've placed a video, you *should* be able to choose an image
from the video as the poster, or still image, that identifies your video
when the video is paused. However, while this works inside InDesign,
InDesign 5.5 forgets to add the code to the HTML file and so it does
not appear in the EPUB file. One workaround is to simply add the
poster image by hand yourself. InDesign similarly lets you designate a
poster for an audio file but does not export that to EPUB either.

And finally, note that while InDesign CS 5.5 automatically adds play
and pause controls to audio files, it does not do so for video. I recommend choosing an option in the Controller menu for a video file (any
option will do) so that InDesign adds controls="controls" to the HTML
which will cause the Play, Airplay, and Full screen icons to appear on
the video file, giving your user some control over when the video plays
(or stops playing).

Note that while you can wrap text around your video or audio files,
InDesign won't export the space around it. To adjust the space around
audio and video files, you'll have to edit your CSS by hand.

Creating links

One of the nice advantages an ebook has over its print counterpart is the ability to fly from one spot in the book to another without having to leaf through to find a specific page. While you can also create links to outside resources (say, a link on a website), these require opening an external application like a web browser and some ebookstores frown on them in general, considering them possible competition! At any rate, I'll focus on links within an ebook from one section to another.

InDesign creates three kinds of intrabook links: hyperlinks, cross references, and footnotes. A hyperlink connects the origin to a marked destination with any text you like. A cross-reference uses the text from the destination as the clickable text—and InDesign will update it if you change the text. A footnote has an automatically-numbered reference that links to the content of the footnote.

Earlier versions of InDesign had a terrible bug that didn't properly generate links in multi-document EPUBs. Thankfully, that issue has been fixed in InDesign CS 5.5 and you can now have a book with several chapters and correctly link between one chapter and the next—or the previous!

Creating hyperlinks

To create a hyperlink, you have to mark the destination first, and then go to where you want the link to appear, and create a hyperlink there.

1 Navigate to the location in your book where the destination of the link should be. Select the bit of text that should appear when the reader clicks the link.

2 Choose Window > Interactive > Hyperlinks to display the Hyperlinks panel if it is not already visible.

3 Choose New Hyperlink Destination from the Hyperlinks panel menu. The selected text appears in the New Hyperlink Destination dialog box.

4 Choose Text Anchor if it's not already selected. You can change the name of the hyperlink if you like, especially if it's very long. (The selected text won't be affected.)

5 Click OK.

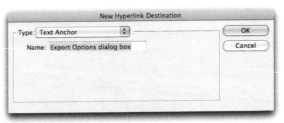

*It's fine to abbreviate or change the Name of the hyperlink destina-
tion to make it easier to remember.*

6 Next, navigate to the place in your book where you want to create the link. Select the text that will be highlighted as a link, the
"clickable" text.

7 This time, choose New Hyperlink in the Hyperlinks Panel menu.
In the New Hyperlink box that appears, choose Text Anchor
from the Link To box at the top and then choose the desired
destination in the Text Anchor box. (This should match what you
had in step 5.)

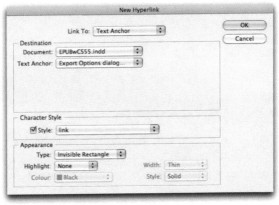

*You can link to destinations in other documents in your book by
choosing them in the Document menu.*

8 If desired, check the Style box and select the character style that
should be applied to the hyperlink.

Creating cross references

Cross references are really great when you want to reference the name or number of a particular section or chapter of your book. You can have InDesign keep track of what that section was called or how that chapter was numbered and update it automatically. For example, you could create a reference like *see Chapter 1 for details*. And if the destination that you choose happens to end up being Chapter 2, the cross reference will automatically change to *see Chapter 2 for details*.

1. To create a cross reference, it's important to make sure that you've styled your destination text properly, particularly with the desired paragraph style.

2. Choose Window > Interactive > Hyperlinks if the Hyperlinks panel is not already showing.

3. Place the cursor where you want the cross-reference to appear. Remember that you will be pulling in text from the destination, and thus if you have anything already selected, it will be replaced with the incoming text.

4. Choose Insert Cross-Reference from the Hyperlinks flyaway menu.

5. In the dialog box that appears, choose either Paragraph or Text Anchor in the Link to box. If you choose Text Anchor, you can reference any hyperlink destination (as created in previous section). If you choose Paragraph, you can reference any styled paragraph.

6. If you've chosen Paragraph, next you'll choose the paragraph style and then the actual paragraph that you want to reference. If you've chosen Text Anchor, you'll now select the one that you want to use. Remember that the name of the Text Anchor sometimes matches its contents, but is not required to do so.

Next choose the Format for the cross-reference. You can decide to use the entire contents of the selected paragraph, or just the number, and you can add text or styling.

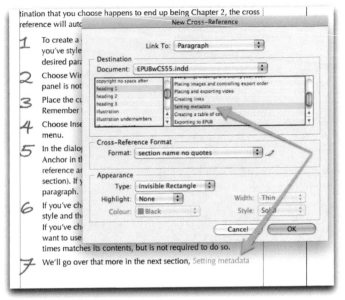

In this example, the Format uses the full text of the paragraph as the cross reference text. You can see what it will look like in the text.

Thankfully, the Appearance Type now seems to have a default value of Invisible Rectangle, which is what I recommend.

 Click OK to complete the cross-reference.

Creating footnotes

Another kind of link that can be very handy in an ebook is footnotes. InDesign can create and lay out footnotes at the bottom of your print pages, and then collect them at the end of a chapter or the end of the book for the digital version.

1 To create a footnote in your book, choose Type > Insert Footnote. The cursor is automatically placed in the space for footnotes which in turn is automatically created at the bottom of the text frame and a numbered superscript appears at the end of the text.

2 Type the contents of the footnote.

Formatting footnotes

Once you have created the footnotes in your book, you can decide how they should be formatted.

1 Choose Type > Document Footnote Options. There are many options for specifying the format in the print book, but we'll skip to the Formatting section, where you can choose the format both for the footnote number as well as for the footnote itself.

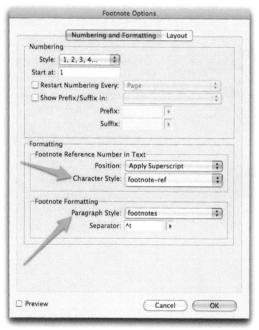

The most important options for the EPUB producer are those that let you set the style both for the footnote reference number and for the footnote itself.

2 Click OK to save the changes.

Finally, you get the choice of whether, when you export the EPUB, the footnotes should follow the paragraph in which they're referenced, or should be collected at the end of the document to which they belong. For more details, see "Navigating the Contents panel" on page 58.

Creating a navigational TOC

One of the characteristics of the EPUB format is that it contains information about the document in a form that ereaders can use to construct an active, or navigational TOC. InDesign can generate this information based on your selection of the styled paragraphs that should be included in that TOC.

1 Before you begin, make sure that your document is properly styled. Create styles for each level of header that you want to include in the TOC and apply them as necessary.

2 Define your navigational TOC by creating a TOC Style. Choose Layout > Table of Contents Styles to designate which paragraph styles should be included. Click the desired paragraph styles in the right panel and then click Add to move them to the Include Paragraph Styles section.

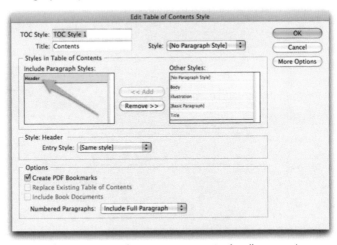

In this TOC, we've chosen to create entries for all paragraphs marked with the Header style.

3 Note the name of the TOC Style, in this example, *TOC Style 1.* You'll need it when you export your EPUB file. You can choose other formatting options as desired, but these will be used only for the TOC in your print book; currently no ereading system allows you to format the navigational TOC.

4 If your book has multiple documents, be sure to choose Include Book Documents at the bottom of the dialog box.

5 Click OK to save the changes.

Now when you export your book to EPUB, InDesign will be prepared to create the navigational TOC according to what you've chosen here.

> ⇒ **Tips** ⇐
>
> If your book has multiple documents, be sure to create the TOC Style in the document that you have designated as the Style Source.
>
> In earlier versions of InDesign, you had to choose a TOC Style upon export in order to map headers to hn elements. Now all paragraph styles are mapped to p elements by default, but you can map them to hn elements as desired manually. (For details, see "Mapping tags to export".)
>
> Another by-product of creating a TOC Style is that anchor ids are automatically added to the paragraph whose styles are included in the TOC Style.

Generating a TOC

Creating a TOC Style does not generate an actual table of contents in your book. To generate an inline table of contents, you must choose Layout > Table of Contents. You'll get a loaded cursor and you'll be able to place the table of contents wherever you like. You are not required to include a table of contents in the body of your ebook unless you'll be exporting to Kindle/mobi. As we mentioned earlier, by defining the TOC Style and choosing it upon export, InDesign can transmit the TOC info to the ereader so that it generates the required navigational TOC for your book. Nevertheless, many books have both a navigational TOC and an actual text one in the body of the book. In earlier versions of InDesign, inline tables of contents would simply disappear upon export. Thankfully, that is no longer the case.

Mapping tags to export

In earlier versions of InDesign, paragraph styles were converted to p elements in the EPUB document, with the style name as a class, by default. In InDesign CS5, if you specified a TOC Style, the elements included in the table of contents were automatically exported as header elements (h1, h2, etc.), again with the paragraph style as a class, while all other elements were exported as p's. InDesign also mapped bulleted and numbered lists to the li element, but didn't do it correctly.

In InDesign CS5.5, all paragraph styles are mapped to p elements by default, but you now have the option to specify the mapping manually. Why would you want to? HTML is designed to be a semantic language, giving meaning to content with specific elements. So a p is just for regular paragraphs but an h1 or h2 is meant for headers. If you have headers, you should map them to header elements. This will not only follow standard HTML practice, but also make them more likely to be read correctly by more ereaders.

Let's imagine a book with these styles:

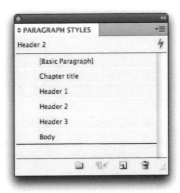

There are two places where you can specify how a paragraph style should be mapped to EPUB, either individually in the Paragraph Style Options panel, or all at once by choosing Edit all Export Tags from the Paragraph Styles panel menu.

Mapping styles individually

1 Open the Paragraph or Character Styles Options dialog box for the style you're interested in. (For example, Control-Click the style name in the panel.) We'll start with the Chapter title style.

2 Click the Export Tagging option at the bottom left of either dialog box. With paragraph styles, you can choose from p or hn elements. Specify a class that should be applied to those elements, if desired. I generally use the ID style name. Click OK when you're finished.

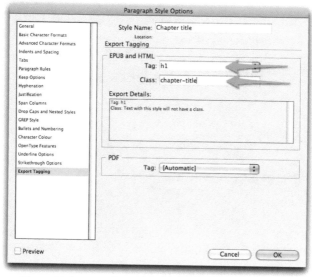

Choose h1 for your Chapter title style since it really is a kind of heading. I use the style name for the class, substituting dashes for spaces (which aren't allowed).

With character styles, you can only choose from span, em, and strong. Again, specify a class if desired.

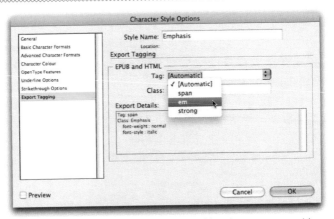

*If your Emphasis character style simply adds italics to your text, it's
better to map it to em. No class is necessary.*

3 Click OK to save the changes.

Mapping all styles at once

If you've got a lot of tags to map, this second method is quicker.

1 Choose Edit All Export Tags from either the Paragraph or
Character Styles panel menu.

2 Click in the Tag area for the style you want to map and choose
the desired option from the menu. Then, if desired, add a class (I
usually use the style name) under the Class menu.

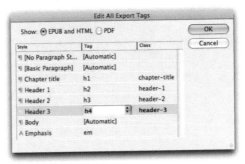

3 Click OK to finish.

Now when you export to EPUB, the Chapter title and each
Header will be mapped to h*n* elements, the rest of the paragraph
styles will be mapped to p elements, and the Emphasis character
style will be mapped to the em element.

Mapping lists

In earlier versions of the software, InDesign basically made a mess of exporting lists. Things have improved greatly in InDesign CS5.5. By default, InDesign will map bulleted and numbered lists to ul and ol elements plus li elements in the EPUB, using the paragraph style as a class. This makes sense. If you don't want InDesign to create ul, ol, and li elements, you can map the corresponding styles as described in the previous sections. Your choices in the Paragraph/Character Styles Option and Edit All Export Tags boxes override the selection that you might make later in the Export panel.

If you map lists to p or hn elements, the automatic bulleting is lost (while the numbering is curiously maintained). To maintain the bullets, choose Convert to Text in the EPUB Export Options box for Bullet Lists upon Export. (See "Margins, lists, and ADE" on page 53.)

Specifying metadata

Before you export your book to EPUB you should specify at least the
most essential metadata, or information about your book, in order to
make it easier for booksellers and customers to find your publication.
The information you specify in the metadata appears both in ebookstores and in ereaders to help identify and describe your books.

There are two places where you can add metadata, in the File
Information box and in the Export Options dialog box. I find it annoy-
ing that they have not been consolidated to a single location.

1 Choose File > File Info to display the File Information dialog
box.

2 At a minimum, enter a Document Title, Author, Description,
Keywords, and Copyright info.

The File Information dialog box.

You'll find additional metadata options, including the all-important one
that includes the metadata in your EPUB, when you go to export your
book to EPUB.

Exporting to EPUB

Adobe has consolidated all of its exporting capabilities into a single Export command. So start by choosing File > Export. Then choose EPUB in the Format menu in the dialog box that appears. Once you have chosen a name and location for your new EPUB file, you will have choices as described in the sections that follow. I will cover them sequentially.

Adding more metadata

You've already seen how to enter some of the metadata for your EPUB, in the "Specifying metadata" section on page 48. In the General section of the EPUB Export Options box, you'll find additional important metadata options.

The Unique Identifier box is where you should enter a book's ISBN.

1 The most important option is the Include Document Metadata box. Check that box or else none of the metadata you added earlier (in the "Specifying metadata" section) will be included in your EPUB file.

2 Enter the Publisher name in the Add Publisher Entry field. Don't add an ampersand to the name, or else the entire field will be ignored, instead use "and". (Thanks @amarie!)

3 If your book has an ISBN, enter it in the Unique Identifier field. If you don't have an ISBN, InDesign will generate a unique number (not an ISBN) for you, as required by the EPUB spec, and will save it (and reveal it) for the next time you export to EPUB.

Note that earlier versions of InDesign did not add information about the date of publication to your book. InDesign CS 5.5 remedies that situation by adding the date metadata automatically. Personally, I'd rather be able to edit that information manually, but I'll take what I can get.

Generating a cover

One of the showier new features of InDesign CS 5.5 is the ability to
include a cover in the exported EPUB file. I showed you how to get a
cover ready earlier in "Creating a cover" on page 21. Now we'll see
how to get that cover into the EPUB.

1 Under EPUB Cover in the General section of the EPUB Export
Options dialog box, choose an option for the cover.

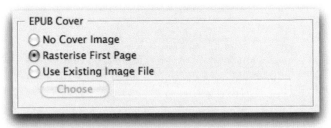

*I'm not sure why I installed the British English version of InDesign,
but that's why it says "Rasterise" instead of "Rasterize".*

The Rasterize First Page option generates a new image file out
of the components of the first page of your book. The code that
InDesign generates to reference the cover is curious. Instead of
creating a separate XHTML file containing this new image, it
simply references the generated image file directly in the *content.opf* file.

```
<metadata>
<meta name="cover" content="x349.png"/>
...
</metadata>
<manifest>
<item id="x349.png" href="images/349.png"
   media-type="image/png"/>
```

This has important ramifications. In Kindle and NOOK, it will
work as expected, but on iBooks the cover image will only be
displayed opposite the Table of Contents and in book lists, but
not as the first page of the book. Instead, the first page of the
book will be the *individual contents* of the cover page, not a
rasterized group.

If you want iBooks to display the new combined cover image as the first page of your book, you have to prepare the image as described in "Creating a cover" on page 21. Then when you export to EPUB, and rasterize that page for the cover, the rasterized image will be used both for the cover icon and also for the first page of the book. Indeed, InDesign creates two separate image files for these two purposes.

2   If you have created a cover in some other program, perhaps Photoshop, click the Use Existing Image File and then click Choose to select the image from your computer. InDesign supports PNG, JPEG, and even GIF format. Again, this will only be used for the cover icon (and opposite the table of contents in iBooks in horizontal position) but not for the actual first page of the book.

3   Choose No Cover Image if you either don't want to use InDesign's cover tools, or you don't want a cover at all. You can always create a cover by hand by following the *Creating the cover* section of my *EPUB Straight to the Point* (pages 113–118 in the print edition).

⇒ Tips ⇐

If you want ADE to be able to generate a proper cover icon, you'll have to edit the *content.opf* file so that it references the XHTML page with the cover image in it, instead of the image itself. Then you'll have to add style="max-width: 100%;" to the img tag that references the cover in that new XHTML page. You can find full details in my *EPUB Straight to the Point* book.

I have also noticed that InDesign adds extra space to the right and left of a grouped cover image. It shouldn't. You can eliminate the space in Photoshop.

Ordering the contents upon export

If you've used the Articles panel to control the order of the contents of individual text frames and objects as described in "Using articles to control export order" on page 29, you'll want to make sure that InDesign uses that order upon export.

Under Ordering in the General Panel in the EPUB Export Options box, you'll find three ways to order the content that is exported to your EPUB file.

Ordering
○ Based on Page Layout
○ Same as XML Structure
◉ Same as Articles Panel

The Ordering section is the third part of the General panel in the EPUB Export Options dialog box.

 Choose Based on Page Layout if you have long text articles in which you've placed anchored images as described in "Using inline objects to control export order" on page 24 and "Custom positioned anchored objects" on page 27.

Choose Same as Articles Panel if you have shorter text frames and independent objects that you have already dragged into order in the Articles Panel as described in "Using articles to control export order".

≫ Tip ≪

For more information about the Same as XML Structure option, see Moving Print Publications to EPUB - Part 1, on Cari Jansen's blog (http://carijansen.com/2010/09/18/moving-print-publications-to-epub/)

Margins, lists, and ADE

The last group of options on the General panel of the EPUB Export Options dialog box is a sort of mishmash, ambiguously called "Formatting Options".

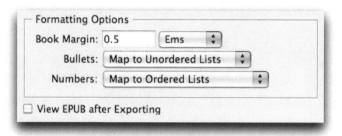

The Formatting Options are a hodgepodge, that, to be honest, I mostly ignore.

The Book Margin option creates an @page rule in the CSS of your exported EPUB that is lovely and standard, but unfortunately ignored by all ereaders except Adobe Digital Editions.

The options in the Bullets and Numbers menus determine whether lists are exported as p elements with whatever class the lists had or as ul or ol and li elements. This option is overridden by any tag mapping that you've already defined (see "Mapping tags to export" on page 44 for details). You can also choose to convert bulleted or numbered lists to text in order to export them as p elements with the bullets or (static) numbers intact.

Finally, you can check (or uncheck as I do) the View EPUB after Exporting, which immediately opens your EPUB in your desktop ereader of choice, like Adobe Digital Editions, assuming you have one installed. Unfortunately, desktop ereaders are not yet very good indicators of how your EPUB will look in ereader devices like the iPad or Kindle, and thus may be more distracting than useful.

Options when exporting images

Let's move on to the Image tab. InDesign has some new revamped
features for exporting the images in your InDesign documents, but it's
not immediately obvious just what all those options do.

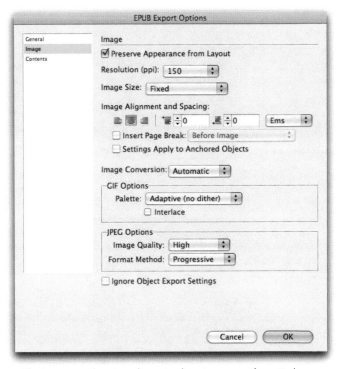

*The Image panel options determine how images are formatted upon
export.*

The first option that you encounter in the Image section is Preserve
Appearance from Layout. This option is roughly equivalent to the
Formatted option in earlier versions of InDesign. What it does is generate a new version of your image that incorporates whatever changes
you have made in the InDesign document with respect to the images'
size, rotation, cropping, effects like drop shadow or inner glow, spacing, and border. InDesign does not add these effects using CSS, but
rather by generating a brand new (static) image file.

The actual pixel dimensions of an exported image are determined both
by the Preserve option as well as the resolution you choose.

If Preserve Appearance from Layout is checked, InDesign calculates the size of the image by measuring the physical size of the image on your layout and multiplying it by the value in Resolution (ppi), as long as the output resolution is smaller than the original resolution. So, an image that measures 3" x 4" on the InDesign page and that is exported at 150 ppi will measure 450 x 600 (3 x 150, 4 x 150) pixels. If the output resolution is higher than the original, the original is maintained.

If Preserve Appearance from Layout is *not* checked, InDesign calculates the final size of the exported image by dividing the chosen resolution (again, as long as its smaller than the original) by the original resolution and multiplying that number by the image's current pixel dimensions. So, suppose you place an image that measures 600 x 800 pixels and has a resolution of 300 ppi and you choose an export resolution of 150. Since 150/300 = 1/2, the pixel dimensions of the exported image will be 300 x 400 (half of the original 600 and 800). If you exported that same image at 400 ppi, the exported dimensions would be the same as the original's: 600 x 800. InDesign doesn't extrapolate up.

Now why would you care what pixel dimensions the images in your EPUB have? For two reasons. First of all, some ereaders have absolute outside limits on the size of the images you place. For example, Apple insists that images be no larger than 2 million pixels. You can get that number by multiplying the height by the width. In the case of 600 x 800, we'd only get to 480,000 pixels so we'd be OK.

The second reason is that some ereaders are very particular about the size of images, especially if these are bigger than the screen size. You may need to adjust the pixel size of your images very carefully to get them to display the way you want.

Note, however, that the intrinsic pixel dimensions of the image are only a part of the battle. Regardless of the size of the image, you can also control the HTML and CSS in order to determine how images are *displayed*.

The code that InDesign uses in the HTML for the image depends on whether you choose Fixed or Relative to Page in the Image Size menu. In the first case, the intrinsic height and width are spelled out with the height and width attributes in the img element right on the HTML page, which results in the image having the exact same pixel dimensions in whatever screen it appears on.

If you check Relative to Page, InDesign calculates the ratio of the size of the image on the InDesign document page with respect to the size of the image's parent element (which would be the whole page for an unanchored object, or just the text frame for anchored objects). InDesign uses the resulting percentage as the value of the width element in the HTML. That means that an image that takes up half of the page in the InDesign document will take up half of an iPad screen page as well as half of an iPhone screen page. This is probably the option you want to use most often.

Well, you would if the perfectly good code that InDesign CS 5.5 creates was properly interpreted by iBooks, which it currently is not. iBooks has a peculiar bug which keeps it from paying attention to percentage widths applied to the img tag. To make it work, you have to adjust the CSS so that the width is applied to the enclosing div and the img tag is set to 100%.

```
div.image {width: 44%}
img {width: 100%}
```

Of course, you can use any width you like, 44% is just an example. If you don't want to edit the CSS file, you have two choices: use exact pixel dimensions or view all your images at 100% of the ereader screen.

Image Size and Alignment

Before you decide what options to choose in the middle section of the Image panel, you should know that there are three sorts of objects in InDesign: inline objects that flow along with the text, anchored objects that are connected to a point in the text but don't move around on the printed page, and independent objects that are not part of a larger text frame, nor are anchored to it. The options chosen in the Image Alignment and Spacing section never apply to the first group and always apply to the last group. If you check the Settings Apply to Anchored Objects, they'll apply to the second group, and if you don't, they won't!

With that in mind, you can also choose an alignment (left, center, or right) and an amount of space to insert before and after the affected images.

The middle section of the Image tab gives you options for formatting the space around your images.

Click Insert Page Break option to add a page break either before, after, or before and after every image. Note that if your book begins with an image and you put page breaks before all images, your book will begin on an empty page.

Image formats

The last section on the Image tab deals with how images are converted. I generally just leave the defaults so that InDesign decides which format to use to get the most efficient and proper compression.

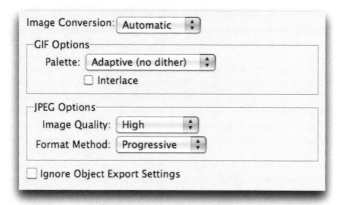

The last option in the box, Ignore Object Export Settings overrides any image conversion settings that you've set for individual objects.

Navigating the Contents panel

Finally, we get to the Contents panel.

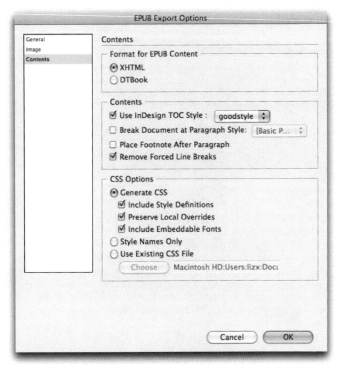

The Contents panel has options for determining how the XHTML, CSS, and TOC are generated.

1 Choose XHTML in the Format for EPUB Content section.

2 In the Contents area, check the Use InDesign TOC Style option and choose the TOC style that you created in "Creating a navigational TOC". If you don't check this option, InDesign creates the navigational TOC from the names of your book's documents.

3 There is still only one absolutely fool-proof way to start a new page: by creating a separate document. Check Break Document at Paragraph Style to divide your book into as many documents as there are instances of the selected style. *All* ereaders will display the first page of a document on a new page. It would be really nice if InDesign let us choose multiple styles on which to divide a book.

4   If your book has footnotes, you can choose to either collect the footnotes at the end of a document (the default) or insert them directly after the paragraph in which the reference appears. For the latter, check Place Footnote After Paragraph. For more details, see "Creating footnotes" on page 40.

5   If you have inserted forced line breaks into your document (Shift-Return) you can have InDesign eliminate them all for you automatically. The only problem is that it simply removes them and does not replace them with anything—like a space—for example. This can create errors if the last word on a line is mashed together with the first word of the following line. Use this feature with extreme caution. (Another way to deal with extra line breaks would be to crack open the EPUB and remove the extra `<br>` tags.)

Looking at the CSS options

The choices you make in the CSS Options area depend on how many similar books you're creating and how expert you are at generating CSS. It's nice that InDesign gives you several choices.

If you don't want to touch the code at all, you should use the first option, Generate CSS. This will have InDesign create a CSS file for you based on the choices you have made when formatting your document. If you have applied styles to your document, you will find these used for the classes of the corresponding p elements. (See "Mapping styles individually" on page 45 for details and exceptions.) The formatting you have chosen for a given style will be defined in that class' CSS—to the best of InDesign's ability.

If you are creating your EPUB for iBooks or Kindle, be sure to uncheck Include Embeddable Fonts, as InDesign's method for doing so is not currently supported by Apple (as described in "Using embedded fonts in iBooks" on page 73) and Kindle doesn't support embedded fonts at all.

InDesign will maintain local formatting unless you specify otherwise.

The second option, Style Names Only is identical to unchecking Include Style Definitions. It is useful if you want to create your own CSS from scratch.

Using Existing CSS

My favorite choice, however, is the third one. When I am creating an ebook, I have InDesign generate the CSS the first time, and then I edit the CSS manually until I'm satisfied with the results. When the content of my book is completed, I then export the EPUB again but instead of using InDesign to generate the CSS, I select my own edited and polished CSS file.

1 Export your ebook the first time using the Generate CSS option.

2 Crack open your EPUB and make any changes necessary to the CSS (as described in "Cracking open EPUBs" on page 61).

3 Copy the entire contents of the CSS file, create a new file, and save it in a new location. You will need this file in the following step.

4 Once your final content is ready in InDesign, export your EPUB from InDesign again, but this time, choose Use Existing CSS file, and then select the file you created in step 3.

5 It may still be necessary to crack open the EPUB and make changes, but you won't have to go back to the CSS file.

Ready to export!

When you've set the Export Options as desired, you're finally ready to click that OK button at the bottom of the dialog box and generate your EPUB file. You can then crack open the EPUB file as I describe in the next section to further customize your ebook and/or convert it to Kindle/mobi format as described in "Converting to Kindle/mobi" on page 68.

Cracking open EPUBs

InDesign can generate a perfectly decent EPUB file, and you could even use that file to generate a perfectly decent Kindle/mobi file. However, because technology moves so quickly and specifically due to the limitations already outlined in "Envisioning your book" on page 7, you may find that you need to open up your EPUB file and make additional changes. While I have tried to focus on InDesign in this book and keep hand-editing to a minimum, there are still very valid reasons for cracking open an EPUB.

Why I still crack open InDesign EPUB files

Over a year ago, I outlined all the reasons why I found it necessary to crack open InDesign-generated EPUB files. With the improvements made to InDesign CS 5.5, I have a few less reasons, but alas, still quite a few. I'll go through the old reasons one by one, explain which ones aren't valid anymore, and then share some new ones.

1 *First and foremost, because the EPUB doesn't validate. To do so, I must add the* dc:date *element.*

Fixed. InDesign CS 5.5 now adds the dc:date element with the date of export, and thus ID-generated EPUB files will now validate. If you want the file to use any other date—or more than one—you'll still have to crack it open.

2 *Because InDesign doesn't properly designate an image or given page as a cover. This is huge!*

As discussed in "Generating a cover", InDesign can rasterize the first page of your book and use it as a cover, but I don't like how it does it. I still crack open EPUBs to specify the cover in a way that ensures that the icon will be generated correctly, and in order to specify the page on which a book should open.

3 *To add metadata. Without standard, accurate metadata, you might as well not publish an ebook because no-one will be able to find it.*

For example, InDesign does not give you a way to include meta-data about multiple authors or their roles, contributors, multiple publication dates, the source of the book. InDesign does have two separate places where some metadata can be introduced. The date is added automatically.

4 *In order to apply text wrap to images and sidebars. Since InDesign supports the creation of text wrap around individual images, groups of images and captions, and sidebars of text, it should also be able to export it into the EPUB (especially considering that only small adjustments in resulting XHTML and CSS are required).*

Thanks to InDesign CS 5.5's improved export of text wrapped images and sidebars, I no longer need to adjust this manually in the CSS.

5 *To wrap text around drop caps.*

InDesign CS 5.5 exports the code for drop caps all right, but it doesn't assign the formatting to the named style that you may have used, opting to create a generic style instead.

6 *To format the first line of text (what in InDesign is a kind of Nested Style) so that it maintains formatting in EPUB.*

InDesign has had this brilliant First Line option in Nested Styles for awhile, but it still does not export it to the EPUB (for example, using the perfectly corresponding CSS pseudo-selector :first-line).

7 *To specify which paragraphs should be kept together, for example, images with captions, headers with first paragraph following, etc. Again, InDesign supports Keep Together in InDesign documents, but doesn't export to EPUB.*

InDesign lets you break a document into smaller documents by choosing a delimiting paragraph style. But it still does not export the information in the Keep Options dialog box, which is a shame, since there is perfectly reasonable CSS code with which to do it.

8 *To specify page breaks. Although iBooks does not yet support page breaks (which is incredible in itself), other ereaders do. This is a major concern of ebook publishers.*

See the previous note.

9 To specify widows and orphans. One more instance where InDesign already has the functionality but does not support it in export to EPUB. Hugely important for ebook publishers (even though not yet supported in iBooks, it is supported by other ereaders).

InDesign still does not export specifications for widows and orphans. And iBooks still doesn't support them. But other ereaders continue to, so InDesign should as well.

10 Because Apple says, on page 15 of their Publishing Guidelines, that "All book elements (for example, the cover, table of contents, first chapter, index, and so on must be identified in the <guide> block." Note the use of the word "must". Note that <guide> is optional according to the current version of EPUB, and Apple has not yet rejected books without <guide> blocks, to my knowledge.

InDesign still does not include any information in the guide block. You still have to do this by hand, for example, if you want to designate where a book should initially open.

11 To add pagination guidelines, so that readers can find passages from a particular page of a print edition in their ebook edition (e.g., in a college class), or so you can create a clickable index.

To my knowledge, InDesign still does not mark the boundaries of a print page in the EPUB document. You must continue to do this by hand.

12 To eliminate erroneous default values that InDesign applies to non-specified properties (which mess up CSS inheritance).

InDesign still specifies a whole series of unnecessary default values.

13 To correct/use font names supported by the iPad.

You still have to adjust the name of Bodoni 72, Bodoni 72 Oldstyle, Bodoni 72 Smallcaps, Bradley Hand, and DBLCDTempBlack. To be honest, I'm not sure if the fault lies with Adobe or Apple.

14 To add Zapf Dingbats (which must be added as UTF-8).

This is still a problem.

15 *To add text in foreign languages, like Hebrew, Arabic, Thai, Chinese, Japanese, etc.*

InDesign CS 5.5 properly exports text in these languages to EPUB.

16 *To fix the spacing bug that occurs when exporting headers (see page 163 in the print edition of my EPUB book).*

This has been fixed.

17 *To force iBooks to support left-aligned text (by inserting a* span *tag within every* p *element). Granted, this is a hack, but text will continue to look really awful when fully justified until we have decent hyphenation dictionaries in ereaders.*

This is still necessary.

18 *To change spacing and margin units from ems to percentages in order to adapt to smaller screens. This is a complicated issue, and will probably get more complicated, but also hugely important.*

InDesign now exports most measurements in pixels. It's still a complicated issue.

19 *To deal with hyphenation.*

This is still an issue.

20 *To fix or insert links. Currently, EPUB export breaks if you try to export a link that contains an ampersand, and most links to Amazon to buy books contain ampersands!*

InDesign now exports links from multiple document books correctly.

21 *To insert video or audio. I would recommend following Apple's lead on this, using HTML5 tags, but allowing for different formats.*

You can embed audio and video into an InDesign document, but see the caveats and notes in "Placing and exporting audio and video" on page 35.

22 *To maintain the inheritance among styles in the InDesign document in the generated styles in the CSS. I know this is complicated, but if I can do it with a little bit of GREP, couldn't ID do it automatically?*

This is still an issue.

New issues

These issues were not on my original list, either because I wasn't familiar with them or because the features were not yet available.

1 *To create a special EPUB file that is designed to convert properly to Kindle/mobi format.*

I will explain some things you need to do to facilitate conversion from EPUB to Kindle in "Converting to Kindle/mobi" on page 68.

2 *To specify the first page a reader should see when she opens the book for the first time.*

Where should a book open the first time? To the cover, to the first page, to the preface, to the table of contents? You can specify where a book should open in the *content.opf* file, but InDesign does not let you set this from inside the program.

3 *To embed fonts*

iBooks and other EPUB ereaders don't have any trouble using embedded fonts, but InDesign doesn't do it in a way that iBooks understands. (Kindle doesn't currently allow font embedding at all.)

4 *To create fixed layout EPUB.*

InDesign CS 5.5 is only useful for creating flowing books. It's really not that much help with fixed layout. I have written two separate miniguides that you might find useful: *Fixed Layout EPUBs for iPad and iPhone* and *Read Aloud EPUB for iBooks* (which turns out to work correctly for Kobo Vox as well).

How do you crack open an EPUB?

An EPUB file is nothing more than a zip file with an EPUB extension. Inside, it contains a *META-INF* folder, a mimetype file, and a folder holding the contents of the book, often, but not necessarily called *OEBPS*. While you can unzip the file to edit the files, there are now a few tools which let you edit the files without having to unzip, which is fairly easy, or rezip, which is a fair bit harder. I recommend BBEdit (for Mac), but the cross-platform oXygen also has this feature. If you want complete details on the inner workings of an EPUB file, I suggest taking a look at my *EPUB Straight to the Point* book.

Opening EPUB files in BBEdit

Choose File > Open and select the EPUB file that you want to open.
You'll see the BBEdit window with the contents of the EPUB listed in
the left pane. By default only "text files" are visible.

That means that you can only see XHTML and CSS files (and the fold-
ers that contain them. To see the *content.opf* and *toc.ncx* files—which
often need to be edited—click the magnifying glass at the bottom of
the left pane, and choose Text Files Only to uncheck it.

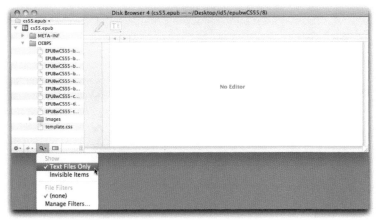

*Click the magnifying glass at the bottom of the left pane and dese-
lect Text Files Only in order to see the* content.opf *and* toc.ncx *files.*

Now all the files will be listed, including the *content.opf* and *toc.ncx* files. To edit a file, simply click its name in the left pane. Its contents will be displayed in the right panel. Make the necessary changes and save as usual; the EPUB file will be modified from the inside, without changing its structure.

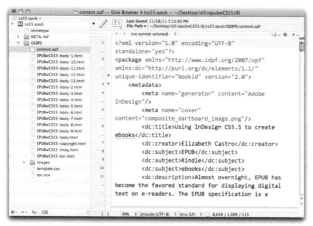

Make any changes you need to the files inside the EPUB.

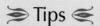 Tips ⋑

You can also right-click a file in the left pane to open it in a new independent window.

Unfortunately, you cannot currently add new files to an EPUB with BBEdit.

The next few sections describe the changes you might want to make to your EPUB file from the inside out.

Converting to Kindle/mobi

Unfortunately, all my wishing to the contrary, Kindle still does not support EPUB directly. Instead, it uses a much simpler, but also HTML-based format called *Kindle*, *mobi* or sometimes *Kindle/mobi*. There are a number of ways to convert an InDesign document into Kindle/mobi format, including a command line program called KindleGen, an export Plugin for Kindle, and finally, Kindle Previewer, which is ostensibly for testing books for Kindle, but turns out to be the best tool for converting them as well.

Note that Amazon announced the more robust Kindle Format 8 format—based on HTML5 and CSS3—in November, 2011, but has released no further details about it. For now, we'll concentrate on Kindle/mobi format.

Creating Kindle-friendly EPUBs

Before you convert an EPUB into the much more basic Kindle format, it makes sense to simplify the formatting so that you don't get any unexpected results. I recommend reading through the Kindle Publishing Guidelines, available from Amazon at http://amzn.to/KPubGuidelines. That document explains just what Kindle/mobi can and cannot handle and how best to format your files. Some of these changes can be made in the InDesign file itself, while others must be carried out by editing the contents of the EPUB file as described in "How do you crack open an EPUB?" on page 65.

Body text

You should not apply any font, font-size, or alignment (e.g., justified, or left-aligned) to normal body text. While you can apply bold, italic, or colors to *selections* of text, you should not apply formatting to the entire body text.

Page breaks

You should not use empty paragraphs to create page breaks. Instead, use InDesign's Break Document at Paragraph Style option to divide the document into smaller pieces or apply the page-break-before and page-break-after properties in the CSS.

Spacing

Body text on the Kindle is indented by default. You can adjust the indent by adjusting the value of the text-indent property in the CSS (or by adjusting the value of Left Indent in InDesign). That said, it doesn't always treat text-indent as you'd (or I'd expect). Test to be sure. And I'll be writing more about Kindle soon. Kindle also supports the margin-top value (Space Before in InDesign).

Text wrap

Kindle does not support the CSS float property and thus it cannot display text wrap, including drop caps. You should eliminate any floats from your CSS for EPUBs destined for Kindle/mobi.

Borders and background color

We've already seen that InDesign won't export borders or background color for any of your book elements, but you can apply the background-color property manually (not background). Regular Kindle will only support it on table elements (table, td, th) but the Kindle Fire accepts it with any text.

Fonts

While Kindle does not currently support embedded fonts, it does have a monospace font that you can use to highlight selections of text. Use the pre, code, samp, kbd, or tt tags in the HTML to format text with a monospace font. Kindle also supports some parts of the font tag, but it has been deprecated for so long that I can't bear to teach you how to use it.

Covers

The preferred size for Kindle ebook covers is 600 x 800px. It should be in JPEG format. The cover must also be present in the body of the book, presumably at the beginning. InDesign CS 5.5's method of inserting the cover is fine for Kindle. Indeed, if you want to create a separate XHTML file for the cover (as I recommend), Kindle asks that you make it non-linear in the spine section of the *content.opf* file.

```
<spine> <itemref idref="cover" linear="no" /> </spine>
```

The cover should also be referenced in the guide section of the *content.opf* file, which should be inserted after the closing </spine> tag:

```
<guide>
<reference type="cover" title="Cover" href="cover.html" />
</guide>
```

Table of contents

According to the Kindle Publishing Guidelines, both a navigational TOC—whose creation I describe in "Creating a navigational TOC" on page 42—and an inline TOC are required in Kindle ebooks. Furthermore, the inline TOC must be found "at the beginning" of the book and should be linked to the corresponding sections of the book. It should not have any page references, since there are no page numbers in a Kindle book.

Even more importantly, the inline TOC must be referenced in the guide section of the *content.opf* file.

```
<guide>
<reference type="cover" title="Cover" href="cover.html" />
<reference type="toc" title="Table of Contents"
    href="EPUBwCS55-toc.html" />
</guide>
```

If you don't reference the TOC in this way, users will get an error when they click the TOC icon (and Amazon may reject your book).

Marking where a book should open

You should specify where a Kindle book should open the very first time a user begins to read it. Some people think this should always be at the very beginning, with the cover or TOC. Others believe that readers will always want to start at the beginning of Chapter 1. It's up to you.

To specify where a book should open the first time, use type="text" in the reference element for the opening document in the guide section of the content.opf file:

```
<guide>
<reference type="cover" title="Cover" href="cover.html" />
<reference type="toc" title="Table of Contents"
    href="EPUBwCS55-toc.html" />
<reference type="text" title="Chapter 1" href="chapter1.html"
    />
</guide>
```

Note that Kindle Fire does not support the standard *text* value for the type attribute. To make Fire open on a given page, use the nonstandard type="start".

Images

Kindle supports GIF, BMP, JPEG, and PNG formatted images, so you'll be fine sticking with what InDesign generates. Amazon asks that you export images in color (not grayscale!) at 300ppi, so that your book will continue to look good in future ereaders. At the same time, Kindle has an upper size limit of 127Kb. Any larger images will be reduced and optimized when you convert to Kindle format. Images that are 127Kb or smaller (that is, optimized by you) are not changed during conversion. Amazon recommends using images at least 600 x 800px and compressing them with a value of 40 or better when saving as JPEG.

Amazon allows text in images as long as the text is not reduced below 7 pixels in size. Books with blurry images or illegible text in images will be rejected.

Converting a Kindle-friendly EPUB to Kindle/mobi

Amazon offers a number of tools for converting your InDesign documents into Kindle/mobi format. First, there is an InDesign Plugin that converts your InDesign documents directly into mobi format. Unfortunately, it has not really kept pace with the EPUB export options available in InDesign CS 5.5 and is pretty limited. I don't recommend using the current version (0.95).

Second, you can use Amazon's KindleGen (available for free from Amazon). However, since KindleGen must be run from the command line, many people find it pretty intimidating.

I discovered a third method from Anne-Marie Concepción. Amazon offers the Kindle Previewer, ostensibly just for testing ebooks on a variety of simulated Kindle devices. But it turns out that when you open an EPUB with Previewer, it automatically converts the file to Kindle/mobi format. The interface is a lot nicer than KindleGen, but the actual conversion is the same.

1 Download Kindle Previewer from Amazon.

2 Choose File > Open and select the EPUB file you want to convert. Consult "Creating Kindle-friendly EPUBs" on page 68 for tips on making EPUB files that convert correctly to Kindle/mobi.

Kindle Previewer will automatically convert your EPUB to Kindle/mobi format and then show it in the Previewer window.

3 Choose the desired Kindle device from the Devices menu to see how your ebook will look in different Kindle apps. It's also a good idea to test your ebook in an actual Kindle (or more than one!)

4 Once you're satisfied with your Kindle/mobi ebook, you're ready to post it to the Amazon store. Start at Kindle Direct Publishing.

Amazon is about to release new KindleGen and Kindle Previewer apps that support KF8. As soon as I have information about them, I will post it to my blog, Pigs, Gourds, and Wikis (www.pigsgourdsandwikis.com).

Using embedded fonts in iBooks

If you are creating ebooks for iBooks (on iPad, iPhone, or iPod touch), InDesign's system of embedding fonts in a book will not work for you. Presumably because of rights issues, InDesign always encrypts fonts when exporting to EPUB. But unfortunately, it does not do it in a way that Apple understands. If you want to embed and use special fonts in your ebook for iBooks, you'll have to adjust the code by hand.

Of course, before you embed fonts in your ebooks, be sure that you have the necessary permission and license to do so. One good place to find free, attractive fonts that are licensed for commercial use is on Google Web Fonts (http://www.google.com/webfonts).

Because BBEdit does not allow inserting new files into an EPUB, you'll have to use Terminal or Springy. (Details in *EPUB Straight to the Point*.)

1 First, InDesign does not include the all important *com.apple.ibooks.display-options.xml* file in the META-INF folder. If you want iBooks to recognize embedded fonts, that file is essential. It's just a text file, with the name as shown, and in its simplest form looks like this:

```
<?xml version="1.0" encoding="UTF-8"?>
<display_options>
   <platform name="*">
     <option name="specified-fonts">true</option>
   </platform>
</display_options>
```

2 InDesign encrypts fonts when it exports them, to protect them against unauthorized copying. To have it work in iBooks, copy the original font to the fonts folder within the OEBPS folder.

3 I have found that sometimes InDesign capitalizes the name of the font in the CSS. Change the name of the font in the fonts folder that you just copied to make sure it matches what InDesign used in the CSS file.

4 Finally, delete the *encrypt.xml* file from the META-INF folder. The font is no longer encrypted, so the file is no longer required.

Additional Resources

I have written a number of publications about creating EPUB ebooks.

EPUB Straight to the Point: Creating ebooks for the Apple iPad and other ereaders (192 pages). Covers the creation of EPUB format ebooks using Word, InDesign (up to CS 5), or from scratch. Gives detailed and complete information on EPUB format itself. Available in print, EPUB format, PDF, and mobi.

Fixed Layout EPUBs for iPad and iPhone, is a 21 page miniguide that focuses exclusively on how to create fixed layout EPUB books. Originally, the code only worked on iBooks, but the new Kobo Vox also supports this specification. Available in EPUB and PDF formats.

Audio and Video in EPUB (29 pages), my second miniguide, gives complete information on including audio and video files in EPUB ebooks. Available in EPUB and PDF formats.

Read Aloud EPUB in iBooks (44 pages), explains how to add an audio track to a fixed layout EPUB file that can be played while the corresponding words in the book are highlighted. Although this miniguide is based on Apple's spec, it is equally valuable for creating Read Aloud EPUB files for Kobo Vox. Available in print, PDF, and EPUB formats.

You can find more information about all my EPUB related publications on my website: http://www.elizabethcastro.com/epub

I post frequently to my curiously named blog, *Pigs, Gourds and Wikis*, about new features, bugs, quirks, and general news about EPUB. You can find it at http://www.pigsgourdsandwikis.com

Anne Marie Concepción's video tutorial, "InDesign CS5.5 to EPUB, Kindle, and iPad" on Lynda.com has a lot of great information. You can get a week's free subscription by following http://lynda.com/freepass/amconcepcion.

While there are a number of websites with increasingly better and more frequent information about EPUB and ebook production, one good way to find them is by following both #eprdctn and myself (@lizcastro) on Twitter. You'll also find a lot of hands-on advice there from people in the trenches.

Index

Made in the USA
Lexington, KY
31 July 2012